Power Writing

A Quick Reference Guide for Managers

Linda G. Lyle, Ph.D.

Avid Readers Publishing Group

Lakewood, California

The opinions expressed in this manuscript are those of the author and do not represent the thoughts or opinions of the publisher. The author warrants and represents that she has the legal right to publish or owns all material in this book. If you find a discrepancy, contact the publisher at www.avidreaderspg.com.

Power Writing

All Rights Reserved

Copyright © 2011 Linda G. Lyle, Ph.D.

This book may not be transmitted, reproduced, or stored in part or in whole by any means without the express written consent of the publisher except for brief quotations in articles and reviews.

Avid Readers Publishing Group

http://www.avidreaderspg.com

ISBN-13: 978-1-61286-019-0

Printed in the United States

FOR KELLY

&

The University of Tennessee's

MBA Class of 2008

"Champions never fade in the stretch"

Power Writing

What Every Manager Needs to Know

FOREWORD: *What is "power" writing, and what's in it for you?*

PART ONE: MASTER THE PROCESS

CHAPTER I	GET THE MEMO	1
CHAPTER II	THE PRE-WRITING PROCESS: Think!	7
CHAPTER III	THE COMPOSITION PROCESS: Core dump	13
CHAPTER IV	THE REVISION PROCESS: Rethink, rewrite, rehabilitate	15
CHAPTER V	THE PROOFREADING PROCESS: Avoid mechanical mishaps	23

PART TWO: MANAGE THE MESSAGE

CHAPTER VI	CONTENT-SPECIFIC TEMPLATES	31
	Executive Summary	33
	Memo of Self-Introduction	34
	Memo to Announce/Initiate Change(s)	39
	Progress Report Memo	41
	Brief Environmental Analysis (SWOT) Memo	42
	Bad News "Bearer" Memo	45
	Guidelines for email	47
CHAPTER VII	DOCUMENTS FOR JOB SEEKERS	49
	Chronological Resumes	50
	Skills-Centered Resumes	52
	Cover Letters	55
CHAPTER VIII	GUIDELINES FOR LONGER REPORTS	57
APPENDIX A	"911" EDITING	64
APPENDIX B	COMPLETE SKILLS RESUME	66

ACKNOWLEDGEMENTS
SUGGESTED REFERENCES

FOREWORD

What is "power" writing?

What's in it for you?

A recent[1] headline in the *Wall Street Journal* read:

STUDENTS STRUGGLE FOR WORDS

Business Schools Put More Emphasis on Writing Amid Employer Complaints

This article prompted literally hundreds of responses, but the comment below is nearly identical to what I frequently hear from professional colleagues, friends, and even my housekeeper:

> *I have worked in HR for many years ... and I find that new grads and even MBAs write the way they talk [and worse]. It's very sad when they can't complete a sentence or explain a simple process. Worst of all, when you try to point out that weak communication skills make bad impressions and damage personal images, they think you're simply insulting them and their B school pedigree. They just don't get it!*

What many people "just don't get" are that writing skills are correlated to personal credibility, and that clear, coherent, concise, and correct writing requires a great deal of painstaking work.

Power Writing assumes that you "get it" and want to "keep it." Even so, this book will not improve your writing skills; that's your job. But it can certainly speed you on your way.

---

[1] March 11, 2011

WHAT IS "POWER" WRITING?

By definition, "power" writing is "good" writing, as opposed to "bad" writing. If you google "good writing," you'll get over 16 million hits -- with no way to discern the sage advice from the downright inane! Even so, it doesn't take an expert to understand that "good" writing is always:

CLEAR. Use precise wording and well-crafted sentence structures to communicate your message as explicitly as possible.

COHERENT. Arrange message units (sentences, paragraphs, sections) in logical orders that enhance the audience's understanding. Note that a message can't be coherent if it's not clear, nor can it be clear if it's incoherent.

CONCISE. Get to the point quickly, support it sufficiently, and move on . Do not waste your words or your reader's time. Even if you're writing an epic novel, you don't want to slobber your story all over the page.

CORRECT. Proofread to perfection. Why? Keep reading.

WHAT'S IN IT FOR YOU?

<u>Good writing is mandatory, but...</u>

According to the Roberts Group, a recent survey revealed that 80 percent of Fortune 1000 executives have chosen not to interview job candidates whose resumes or cover letters used incorrect grammar, spelling, or punctuation. Of those same executives, 99 percent said that poor writing skills often hurt employees' chances for promotion. In fact, effective communication skills are "must haves" for managers and employees alike, and "effective writing" tops most charts as a manager's most valuable skill. One CEO even declared that clear written communication must be a core competency of any business entity[2].

---

[2] Sun Microsystems former and formidable CEO, Scott McNealy.

Ironically, however, **writing** is often rated "below expectations" in performance reviews, and employers spend "billions" _every year_ to correct writing deficiencies, according to a survey of 120 major American corporations affiliated with Business Roundtable[3].

Good writing is cost-effective.

A U.S. Navy self-assessment determined it could save $27 million to $57 million a year if officers wrote clear, coherent memos – simply because of the excess time it takes to plow through garbled verbiage. Similar savings could be realized in the private sector if it stressed good writing skills.[4]

Good writing enhances personal "power."

Perhaps the best argument for good writing is the most obvious: _People are influenced only by what they understand._ Put another way, a "lost" audience is never persuaded of anything. The better you write, the better you are understood and thus the more likely you are to influence others; the more you influence others, the more "powerful" you become.

Bottom line:

Personal success is highly correlated to good (powerful) writing skills. The purpose of this book is to help kick your skills into power mode, and thus to enhance your quality of life, at work and everywhere else. Seriously.

WHAT DOES THIS BOOK DO?

Metaphorically speaking, writing may be compared to a two-engine aircraft. One engine drives the mechanics that produce the manuscript; the other engine drives the clarity and impact of your message. Both engines must be fully functional to avoid costly mishaps. This book:

[3] http://www.collegeboard.com/prod_downloads/writingcom/writing-ticket-to-work.pdf
[4] http://www.editorialservice.com/11ways.html

Helps you master the mechanics

- Explains the writing process in a series of easy-to-follow steps that you can use as a model for your own writing tasks;

- "Zeros in" on the most common problems writers face and provides simple but effective solutions;

- Serves as a quick reference guide for common questions about writing.

Helps you manage the message(s)

Unlike many reference books, *Power Writing* contains templates for and examples of common business documents. How does a memo differ from an Executive Summary? As a "new boss," how can you create goodwill in a memo of introduction? How can a "power memo" initiate change both positively and sincerely? This booklet can help you compose these and other commonly-used business documents.

In short, *Power Writing* provides a quick, no-frills reference for busy professionals (and anyone) who understand that the quality of one's writing can "make or break" job offers, incomes, raises, promotions, teams, departments, entire companies – and most of life in general.

PART ONE

MASTER THE PROCESS

CHAPTER I: GET THE MEMO!

Offhand references to "getting the memo" are as common as computers in most workplaces. So are memos themselves, be they electronic or otherwise. This chapter outlines the basic memo's format; subsequent chapters provide templates and models for various business memos.

MEMOS "R" FORMATS

<u>What is a memo ?</u>

The term "memo" refers to a general format. To use this format:

- Center the word "Memo" or "Memorandum" atop the page.
- Use a single-spaced header (To, From, Re, Date).
- Avoid taking up half the page with the above two items.
- Write <2 pages.
- Write paragraphs containing <8 lines of type.
- Use either *Times New Roman or Arial*, 11 or 12 point font.
- Allow either 1" or 3/4" on all sides.
- If you need more space, EDIT. Do not decrease font size.
- Use single-spaced *block style exclusively.*

What is "block" style vs. "paragraph" style?

- BLOCK STYLE is characterized by
    - single spaced sentences within paragraphs
    - double-spacing between paragraphs
    - lack of indentation (do not indent!)

    Block style is used for all memos.

- PARAGRAPH STYLE is characterized by
    - double-spaced, indented paragraphs
    - one double space between paragraphs (not two)

    Paragraph style is appropriate for longer reports.

What else must a memo contain?

- **Topic headings.** The memo body MUST be divided into sections, each labeled with the appropriate topic heading. Sections may contain one or more paragraphs. If graphics (e.g. charts) are included in the memo, it is normally appropriate to "wrap" text around the graphics or to attach them as appendices.

- **Introductory remarks.** In memos, introductory "paragraphs" are normally limited to a brief statement (1-2 sentences) of the memo's purpose, but introductions may also contain brief background remarks, where warranted/required. Regardless, introductions should be <4 typed lines. Some memos do not need an introduction.

- **Conclusions.** Please do not confuse the meaning of "conclusion" as in "an ending" with conclusions as "results or findings." Here, we mean "ending."

Caveat: Memo formats can vary widely and are often determined by corporate customs and/or preferences.

<u>The Memo Double-Check List</u>

When you think you're totally finished and feel that you couldn't edit another word if your career depended on it, force yourself to take one last "swipe" at proofreading by using this checklist.

- Use the correct format.
- Begin the memo with a purpose statement.
- Include topic headings.
- Use spell check; then, hunt down homonyms.
- Use "it" instead of "they" to refer to a company.
- Remember: "this" cannot stand alone; "this" should modify a noun.
- Beware the ides of "it" -- it what?
- Use parallel structure in lists and/or bullet points.
- IN GENERAL, use active wording instead of passive.
- Avoid vague references and sweeping generalizations.
- "Lean" your prose. Avoid awkward/wordy constructions.

FINALLY, take a look at: http://www.copyblogger.com/5-common-mistakes-that-make-you-look-dumb/

A model memo appears on the next page; is your memo's format identical to the model's? It should be.

MODEL MEMO FORMAT

TO: Dr. Linda Lyle, CEO

FROM: Good Writer

RE: Personal leadership qualities

DATE: November 7, 2010

Thank you for the opportunity to describe my leadership qualities and to discuss how I developed these skills.

Role Models

I was fortunate to grow up in a family with many excellent role models, especially my parents who have always been my greatest supporters. From my father, I learned the importance of competitiveness and a strong work ethic. As a private contractor in waterline construction, farmer, and former State Representative, he has worked diligently and has been an effective leader in his community for many years. My father offers support by sharing his numerous resources, offering advice, and discussing past experiences, all of which have benefited my personal and professional growth.

My mother is an exceptionally caring and giving person. From her, I learned the importance of loyalty and sacrifice. She has always placed our family's needs above her own and made personal sacrifices to take care of her children, parents, and in-laws at various times throughout their lives. Her support continues to have an impact on my life and has been extremely beneficial in my leadership development. Because of my parents' teachings and support, I have learned the importance of hard work, competitiveness, and loyalty and have used these traits to become an effective leader.

Former Supervisors and Management Style

Two of my former supervisors have made a lasting impression on me. Mike Keeler, my boss at Tennessee Consolidated Retirement System (TCRS), stressed the importance of thinking independently while working within a team setting. Mike set a good example by finding a way to integrate autonomy, teamwork, and supervision in our workplace.

As a graduate assistant for the XXX basketball team, I worked for Coach XXX and saw firsthand the importance of teamwork, effective communication, and respect. Coach surrounded herself with hard working, loyal people who respected others and demanded respect for themselves. My management style reflects many of the principles that I learned from these mentors: hire honest and loyal people, set high expectations, offer direction but also autonomy, respect yourself and others, and demand everyone's best effort.

Impact

My role models and former bosses helped develop skills and values that have been invaluable throughout my career. As a member of the Equity Sector Fund team at TCRS, I communicated effectively with my coworkers and Wall Street analysts and worked long hours to outperform my benchmark. In that position, I increased my client base by 20% annually. Additionally, as a graduate assistant, I was praised for my loyalty, sacrifice, and hard work, which enabled me to assist in the coordination and direction of four basketball camps and over 2,000 campers. I am confident that these skills will continue to enhance my career in management.

CHAPTER II: THE PRE-WRITING PROCESS
Develop and practice your "kickoff" strategy

Cut to opening clip: A befuddled face stares blankly at an empty computer screen and wails, **"I don't know where to start!"** Sound familiar?

"Screen fright" is not caused by an inability to *write,* but by an inability to *pre-write.* Seasoned writers typically develop a pre-writing routine to "kick off" their projects.

Less experienced writers may have problems if they don't have a kickoff process to kick off the process. So, here's a process you can use until you find your preferred kickoff routine.

First, bear in mind that pre-writing should take roughly twice as much time as writing the actual document. Read that sentence again.

More specifically, plan to spend your time as follows:

- 30-40% PRE-WRITING
- 10-20% WRITING THE FIRST DRAFT
- 40-50% REVISING, EDITING & PROOFING

Do you find these numbers shocking? If so, tighten your seat belt; you're in for another jolt or two. If not, keep driving; you're on the right road, and the fog will clear momentarily.

What takes so much time? In a word: thinking. In the pre-writing process, you basically "think up" what to write, as well as how to arrange your thoughts.

Put another way, if writing were a football game, then the "draft' is analogous to the 60-minute contest, whereas prewriting and editing alike are more akin to the hours and hours of pre-game planning and practice.

But that's football. How do you plan to for a rough draft?

RULE 1: DO NOT START WRITING!

First and foremost, the power writer THINKS. Powerful writing begins with these thought processes:

- Brainstorming
- Gathering and categorizing data
- Identifying an explicit purpose
- Analyzing the audience

BRAINSTORMING

Grab a notepad (electronic or paper) and list every idea you can think of that is relevant to your writing task. Google "brainstorming for writing" and you'll come up with over 1.5 million results. Many of these will walk you through various brainstorming procedures. One of my favorite sites is:

http://www.unc.edu/depts/wcweb/handouts/brainstorming.html

If the website's purpose is to help generate ideas, then it's likely a useful site. The point is to generate as many "line items" as you can. You may begin to see categories (i.e. related items) emerge, but for now, ignore those; just add to your list whatever thoughts come to mind. You should take away from this first step more ideas than you can possibly use.

Here's another approach. Picture your ideas as if they were multi-colored candies that you have fished out of a 10-pound bag of trail mix. Once you have found all the candy you want, stand back and look at the mix. What do you notice right away? Probably that you have different color groups. Likewise, your brainstorming ideas can be grouped together. For now, be aware that:

- Some ideas may not seem to fit in at all; that's ok.

- As one idea leads to another, you may end up with several different brainstorm lists! Choose the one that is most promising, and move on.

GATHERING AND CATEGORIZING DATA

By this time, you should have a rudimentary grasp of your document's potential content. Some documents (reports and such) require that you gather data; others (personal statements and such) do not.

Regardless, now is the time to look at your brainstorming list(s); if you have more than one, choose the one that most appeals to you. Then, try to separate your ideas (candy) into similar topics (colors); that is, look over your brainstorm list and put similar ideas together. You'll begin to see topics or categories emerge as you think through this part of the process.

Soon, you will reach a fork in the road, and you must take it.[5]

1. If you are writing a letter or memo that needs little-to-no hard data (such as a memo of self-introduction), then look at your brainstorm list and divide it into "piles" of similar thoughts. Then, label these piles. For example, one pile might be "why I'm glad to have this opportunity;" others might be "my background" or "my leadership philosophy." Sort the "candies"/ideas into their proper color/topic groups. You may have an idea or two that match nothing; set them aside, but don't discard them yet.

2. If you need data, find enough to support the ideas you've categorized (a.k.a. RESEARCH). Then proceed as suggested above.

If you have more than 3-4 categories for a 1-2 page memo or letter, then you need to rethink your categories and either divide them more generally – or rank order the categories in order of importance and throw out the "losers." Likewise, if you have fewer than 2-3 categories, then you need more data to categorize!

Finally, arrange your categories in a logical order. For memos or other short papers, simply put yourself in the reader's place and ask, "What would I want to know first, next, and so-forth?" Make sure that one category logically follows another. Different types of order are discussed in most writing textbooks.

---

[5] Apologies to Yogi Berra.

IDENTIFYING A SPECIFIC PURPOSE

Armed with categorized data, you are now ready to decide upon a specific purpose.[6]

Suppose an investment club asks you to recommend a candy stock that pays dividends, and after several brainstorming and data-gathering sessions, you select the *Tootsie Roll* company.

Your general purpose is to *persuade* people to behave in a certain way.

Your specific purpose is to convince your audience to purchase stock in the *Tootsie Roll* company.

See the difference in *general* vs. *specific* purposes? Thought so.

Now, ask yourself: What would motivate my audience to buy *Tootsie Roll* stocks? Before answering this question, you must know something about your audience (a.k.a. audience analysis).

ANALYZING THE AUDIENCE

Try to put yourself inside the minds of your audience. How would you want them to approach you, if you were in their place? Before you write, generate some empathy; you may want to use these questions as a starting point:

1. Who are they (demographically)?
2. Why should they read your document?
3. What is your relationship with them?
4. How much do they know about your topic?
5. How will they likely react to your message?
6. Do you speak "their" language?
7. Is your tone appropriate for this audience?

---

[6] Many writers prefer to complete this process immediately after brainstorming. Your call.

One trick that some writers find helpful is to picture in their heads one of their readers and pretend they are writing to that person.

The goal is to connect with your audience!

CHAPTER III: THE COMPOSITION PROCESS

From Core Dump to Coherent Discourse

Hard to believe, but this section is the shortest in the manual – just as the actual writing you do for any document should be the least time-consuming part of the whole project. Why? Remember: the hard labor should come during the PREWRITING and REVISION steps. Revision and proofreading (editing) should consume from 40-50% of the writer's time on any given project. If you don't complete each step in turn, then you're likely to lose yourself in a maze from which you may never emerge!

<u>**You are now ready to write!**</u> **Armed with your outline and/or list of topics, write straight through the first draft.**

"Core dump" your brain. Do not get distracted. Just WRITE.

No matter how lost you feel, keep writing until the entire paper, chapter, or appropriate segment is complete. Remember to use your topic notations (PRE-WRITING) as a guide.

DO NOT STOP TO EDIT.

When you're finished, you'll have a mess. Walk away from it, for at least an entire day. Only then should you begin the revision process; soon, you'll see a coherent message emerging from the initial core dump! ☺

CHAPTER IV: THE REVISION PROCESS

Rethink, Rewrite, Rehabilitate

Revision is probably the most important step in writing effectively. Revision is the process that transforms your original thoughts into a document that is coherent, clear, and correct. Processes are strategic by definition; thus, revisions should be strategic instead of haphazard.

1.0 START WITH A COMPLETE ROUGH DRAFT

Effective revision always begins with a complete rough draft, no matter how rough it might be! Do not try to revise as you write your first draft: simply put all your thoughts on paper. Only after you have completed this step should you begin to revise!

2.0 EXAMINE PARAGRAPHING

2.1 Are paragraphs unified?

That is, do they address one major topic and contain sufficient explanatory and/or supporting details? Avoid cluttered and confusing paragraphs. Get to the point, make it, support it, and move on.

2.2 Are paragraphs coherent?

Do sentences in the paragraph link smoothly to the proceeding and following sentences? To achieve coherence, use transitional words & referent pronouns, repeat key words appropriately, and/or use parallel structure, Also, eliminate content that is extraneous or off topic.

2.2.1 LINKAGE is also an important issue for the entire document. Relevance to the purpose should be evident in every word!

2.3 Are paragraphs appropriate in length?

- In business writing, standard paragraph length should fall into the 60-80 word range.
- Complex topics need to be divided into several paragraphs, even if they fall under the same topic headings (see section on memo formatting in Chapter I).
- Be aware of the visual effects of paragraphing and avoid walls of text.

3.0 EXAMINE SENTENCE STRUCTURE

3.1 Avoid separating complete sentences with a mere comma.

SPLICE:

Spring has sprung, summer will be along soon!

HOW TO CORRECT:

(1) Separate the two sentences with an end mark or semi-colon, or with a coordinate conjunction such as and, so, or, but, nor:

Spring has sprung, so summer will be along soon!

(2) Subordinate one of the clauses:

Since spring has sprung, summer will be along soon!

3.2 Use fragments only sparingly, for effect.

☹ *When the bond market fails.*

☺ *When the bond market fails, we're toast!*

3.3 Avoid dangling and/or illegal constructions.

☹ *Buried underneath a pile of dust for 40 years, he found all the records intact.*

Hold on! The <u>person</u> who found the records wasn't buried, as this passage suggests. Rethink.

☺ *He found all the records intact, even though they'd been buried under a pile of dust for over 40 years.*

☺ *The records buried under a pile of dust for over 40 years were found intact.*

3.4 Avoid mixed structures. Parallel constructions = clarity!

☹ *We came home and enjoyed dinner and then we watched TV.*

☺ *We came home, enjoyed dinner, and then watched TV.*

3.4.1. Lists must also be parallel. These rules apply to lists in context as well as to bulleted lists.

☹ *When you put together a business report, include time for cover page presentation, organizing a table of contents, and writing an executive summary.*

☺ *When you put together a business report, include time for preparing a cover, organizing a table of contents, and writing an executive summary.*

3.5 Avoid other common sentence errors:

- Awkward phrasing
- Needless repetition
- Garbled, imprecise passages
- Non-sequitur problems
- Not on topic
- Excess verbiage

3.6 Use a variety of sentence types and patterns.

Simple: *She prepared the report yesterday. We read it today.*

Compound: *She prepared the report yesterday, and we read it today.*

Complex: *Although she prepared the report yesterday, we didn't read it until today.*

3.7 Try this method for taming unruly prose:

- Circle the prepositions; revise to eliminate as many as possible.
- Circle "be" or "is" verb forms; replace these with action verbs.
- See *Appendix A* for the rest of the "911 Editing" process.

4.0 CHOOSE EFFECTIVE WORDS

4.1 As a rule, use short and simple words.

☹ *To recapitulate, our utilization of incorrect procedures precipitates interminable delay.*

☺ *To review, incorrect procedures cause endless delay.*

4.2 Use specific, concrete language.

☹ *The computer broke down several times recently.*

☺ *The MBA server broke down three times last week.*

4.3 Avoid clichés, slang, and buzz words, as a general rule.

4.4 Avoid redundancy, or unnecessary repetition.

☹ *Signing both copies of the contract is a necessary requirement.*

☺ *Please sign both copies of the contract.*

4.5 Avoid wordiness! (See Appendix A).

    4.5.1 Substitute one or two words for phrases were possible

  ☹ *In view of the fact that the model failed twice during the time we tested it, we are searching for other options.*

  ☺ *Because the model failed twice during testing, we are searching for other options.*

4.5.2 Don't hide verbs inside pedantic noun phrases.

Instead of:	Use:
Arrived at the conclusion	concluded
Came to an agreement	agreed
Gave a demonstration	demonstrated
Held a meeting	met
Performed an analysis of	analyzed

4.5.3. Don't obscure the subject.

☹ *There was no indication that it was necessary to include John in the meeting.*

☺ *No one indicated that John should be included in the meeting.*

4.6 Avoid excessive and/or unnecessary jargon.

☹ *Your incorrect billing was caused by a computer virus which disabled the error lockout function, resulting in encrypted data.*

☺ *A software glitch created incorrect billing.*

4.7 The use of first and second person in business documents is not only correct but usually preferred, *so long as these points-of-view are used correctly.*

5.0 REVISE FOR APPROPRIATE TONE

5.1 As a general rule, use positive language.

☹ *We cannot ship your computer until we receive your payment.*

☺ *As soon as we receive your payment, we will ship your computer.*

(In short, stress what can be done rather than what cannot be done.)

5.2 Use courteous language.

5.3 Use appropriate voice/person.

5.4 Assume the "you attitude;" put yourself in your audience's place.

6.0 PROOFREAD FOR GRAMMATICAL ERRORS

See the next section for help in avoiding commonly-made mistakes.

CHAPTER V: THE PROOFREADING PROCESS

Avoid mechanical mishaps

Let's face the truth: grammatical errors adversely affect the writer's credibility. Common gaffes include:

1.0 STRATEGIC ERRORS

Avoid the most obvious error of all: failure to proofread aloud. Better still, find someone who is willing to proofread your work, just as professional writers do!

2.0 AGREEMENT ERRORS

2.1 Avoid subject-verb disagreement.

    2.1.1. Beware of intervening prepositional phrases.

    ☹ *The box of recordings date back to 1940.*

    ☺ *The box of recordings dates back to 1940.*

    2.1.2. Each word below is singular and takes a singular verb.

            Anybody
            Anyone
            Everybody
            Everyone
            Nobody
            No one
            One
            Somebody
            Someone

2.1.3. Each of these constructions is likewise singular:

Each (of)

Either … or and either (of)

Neither … nor and neither (of)

One (of)

2.1.4. Collective nouns are treated as a SINGULAR unit:

Company, class, committee, family, government, management, team, and panel are common examples.

2.2 Avoid pronoun-antecedent disagreement

2.2.1. Impersonal pronouns (it, their) can cause trouble!

☹ *The university lost their basketball coach.*

☺ *The university lost its basketball coach.*

2.2.2. Note that the list in 2.1.2. above is applicable to pronoun-antecedent agreement as well.

2.2.3. Avoid vague pronoun reference; antecedents must be clear and unambiguous

Vague:

They said it would rain (who said?).

This is stupid (this what?)

Jane spoke to Linda as she walked (who walked?).

Most uses of the word "it"

3.0 USAGE ERRORS

3.1 Avoid confusing homonyms. Common examples include:

    3.1.1. accept = active verb; except = with the exception of

I will accept all forms of payment except cash.

    3.1.2. affect = active verb; to act upon;

        effect = noun; results of affects

The budget cuts will adversely affect the department.

Your program will see no harmful effects.

*Confusing exception: EFFECT can also be used as a verb, as in "to effect change." Here, the meaning is broader in scope than merely affecting someone or something. To be on the safe side, ignore this exception.

    3.1.3. principal = (a) sum of money or (b) a primary factor, or

        (c) a school official.

        principle = rule or ethic

"The Constitution's guiding principle is equality, but its principal applications are found in Supreme Court rulings," said the principal.

3.1.4. cite = to quote or mention

site = place (also website)

sight = seeing

The sight of a landfill overtaking the forest was disgusting.

The site of my former high school is now a strip mall.

He cited the city's right of imminent domain to seize the property.

3.2. Avoid confusing possessives such as:

Their = belonging to them

They're = they are

There = a place opposite here

Your = belongs to you

You're = you are

It's = it is

Its (no apostrophe) = belongs to it

4.0 COMMAS & OTHER PUNCTUATION DEMONS

4.1 Commas

Use a good reference book to sort out comma rules. *Avoid the "rule" that a comma should be used every time a reader or speaker would pause. That's not a rule.* The most important rules to remember:

4.1.1. Use to separate items in a series.

Most MBAs major in marketing, finance, or logistics.

4.1.2. Use to separate independent clauses joined by a co-ordinate conjunction (and, but, or, nor).
The air was hot, and the ground was dry.

4.1.3. Use after introductory phrases/clauses

Because of campus policies, we can't bring beer to class.

4.2 Do not over-use semi-colons.

These marks are used most often (1) to separate complete sentences that are closely related, and (2) to separate phrases or clauses in a series. Examples:

(1) The stock market rose; the bond market fell.

(2) Take your clothes to the laundry; fill up the gas tank; and stop at the grocery store for milk, bread, and butter.

4.3 Use colons correctly; avoid over-use.

4.3.1. Use to introduce explanations that are preceded by an independent clause.

☺ *Don't forget: you may need a recommendation.*

4.3.2. Use prior to a bulleted or in-text list.

4.4 Use ellipses [. . .] only when part of a quotation is omitted.

    Do not use interchangeably with dashes.

4.5 Write out numbers ten and under; use numerals 11>

4.6 Direct and indirect quotations

    Indirect: Jane said that it was time for lunch.

    Indirect: Did Jane say, "Lunch time!" ?

    Direct: Jane said, "Lunch time!"

5.0 ACTIVE vs. PASSIVE VOICE

As a general rule, use active voice [subject is acting] instead of passive voice [subject is being acted upon].

    Passive: The computers were updated by the tech crew.

    Active: The tech crew updated the computers.

Although it should be used sparingly, passive voice is appropriate when:

- You don't know the actor: *The MBA lounge was robbed.*
- You don't want to point fingers: *The billboard was defaced.*

6.0 OTHER COMMON ERRORS AND WHERE TO FIND HELP

CAPITALIZATION. Have you been looking for this section? You won't find it here, chiefly because capitalization rules are in a state of such flux that your best bet is to consult a reliable, contemporaneous web source. My recommendations:

http://www.scribd.com/doc/2664713/Associated-Press-AP-Style-Guide-the-basics

http://owl.english.purdue.edu/owl/resource/592/1/

You may be plagued by "demons" that are not included here. If so, purchase a standard handbook for more detailed references, examples, and exercises. (Try that before hiring a tutor, anyway!) Suggestions:

- *American Psychological Association (APA) Handbook*
- *Modern Language Association (MLA) Handbook*
- *Harbrace Handbook*
- *Associated Press (AP) Style Manual*
- Strunk & White, *Elements of Style*

PART TWO

MANAGE THE MESSAGE

CHAPTER VI: CONTENT-SPECIFIC MEMO TEMPLATES

THE EXECUTIVE SUMMARY

<u>What is an Executive Summary?</u>

This document is just what the term implies: it is a *summary* of a longer report's contents, normally written in memo format (see above).

Typically, the Executive Summary

- Overviews major findings, conclusions, and/or any appropriate recommendations included in the longer report.

- Is organized using the same topic pattern as that of the longer report.

- Varies in length, depending upon the length of the report it summarizes.

- Should be a one page, single-spaced document that contains topic headings – just like any other memo.

<u>What is the difference between a memo and an Executive Summary?</u>

- The *Executive Summary is merely a memo*, predicated upon content.

- A *memo* is simply a format that may be used with a plethora of document types, including Executive Summaries, email messages, proposals, meeting minutes, short analyses, and the like.

MEMO OF INTRODUCTION

Congratulations! You have your dream job: you're a manager, supervisor, or even a C-suite executive. If you're new to the company, rest assured that virtually everyone in the organization wonders who you are, what you believe, and how you operate. If you have been promoted from within, your new subordinates wonder how you will approach your new role.

Why not dispense with a few key issues and create a tad of goodwill for yourself on Day One? A carefully-crafted memo can do just that.

The core goals of this memo are (1) to make a positive first impression – or at least one that will accrue the benefit of doubt; and (2) to give your audience its first taste of your leadership style.

Use the following guidelines when composing this memo.

- CAREFULLY consider your audience!
    - Put yourself inside their heads.
    - What might they reasonably hope or expect from you?
    - What do they want to know about you? What do they need to know? These two answers aren't the same.

- Watch the tone and attitude you communicate. Both are engendered by your language.

- Make sure that your memo:

    - paves the way for a positive beginning

    - avoids overstating or understating personal info

    - clearly considers the audience

    - avoids overemphasis on directives

    - (where needed) alludes to concerns without "dissing" the past

    - is upbeat and enthusiastic, as appropriate

    - evidences an approachable personality

    - reeks of collegiality (e.g. "We're all in this together.")

On the following pages, you will find two model memos.

Memo A is from a newly-hired regional manager who will supervise the current plant managers of a well-respected manufacturing company.

Memo B is from a hospital's new CEO who was promoted from within after the previous CEO was terminated, chiefly because he alienated most of the hospital's physicians.

Feel free to use and/or to combine these memos' wording to help write your own entre, should you wish to do so.

NEW BOSS: MODEL MEMO A

TO: Parker Manufacturing Plant Managers

FROM: [YOUR NAME & TITLE]

RE: A personal introduction

DATE: September 20, 2012

The purpose of this memo is to introduce myself and to share a few thoughts about my role as a newly-appointed Regional Manager. First, however, please accept my congratulations for your well-earned reputation for excellence. I am both honored and eager to join Parker's team!

Professional Background

My career in the Machine Tooling industry began in 1989 when I held a part-time job working on the plant floor for a local seat-belt manufacturer. In 1992, I earned the Bachelor's Degree in Industrial Engineering from Northwestern University; then, I worked for Nexis, a small manufacturer of belt grinders in the Chicago area. I spent six years on the Nexis design team before moving into operations management. After serving for two years as an Assistant Plant Manager, I was tapped to manage a new Nexis facility in Champaign, Illinois, a position I have held for the past six years.

Why Parker?

I have always admired Parker Manufacturing's impressive growth and sterling reputation. Total revenue increased more than 10% in each of the last five years, and most of that progress is a direct result of your hard work. You have also done an outstanding job of increasing plant efficiency while maintaining an impeccable safety record. Further, employee turnover at the plant level is at an all-time low compared to industry standards, which illustrates your commitment to this organization. And you are eager to achieve even higher standards of excellence.

Our Goals

As you know, Parker is positioned to continue its growth and to gain market share. Our goal is to double company-wide revenue over the next five years by increasing sales to our existing customers, attracting new customers, and expanding geographically. Additionally, we will need to control costs at the plant level in order to sustain acceptable profit margins. These tasks will not be easy, given the state of the economy, but I have confidence that by working together, we will attain these goals.

My Role

Put simply, my role is to support you in every possible manner. I believe in a collaborative working environment and open communication, so I will request input from each of you on a regular basis. I will also maintain an open-door policy and encourage you to contact me whenever I may be of service. I see great potential in this group, and I look forward to touring your plants next week at the times you have scheduled. I also look forward to earning your trust and to our building a fruitful relationship.

Meanwhile, if you have any questions or concerns, please feel free to contact me at any time at (865) 391-0061 or dedelson@parkermanufacturing.com.

NEW BOSS: MODEL MEMO B

TO: Ventura Hospital Medical Staff

FROM: [YOUR NAME & POSITION]

RE: Introduction

DATE: March 5, 2011

Hello everyone! I am very excited about this unique opportunity to serve as your CEO, and I am looking forward to working with all of you.

Personal History

I worked my way through college as a hospital orderly. This initial exposure to medicine piqued my interest in healthcare, and taught me, among other lessons, the critical role of communication in providing quality patient care. As many of you know, I practiced as an orthopedic surgeon for many years until I became interested in the administrative side of medicine. I then earned my MBA, and for the past two years, I have served as a junior administrator here at Ventura.

Possible Concerns

Having been on the scene, I understand the several problems that existed between the former C-suite and the hospital's medical staff. However, today I ask that we begin that relationship anew. As CEO, I will remain first and foremost a team player. This hospital's mission is to provide excellent care for patients, which happens only when all administrators and medical staff understand that we must all work together. Specifically, we must share our ideas, listen to each other's concerns and make collaborative decisions. As a physician, I understand the pressures that come from providing patient care, dealing with insurance companies, and not least, in trying to balance work-life stresses. Thus, one of my admittedly unusual goals as your CEO is to help you manage these issues, where possible.

Initial Plans

I plan on having several "Town Hall" meetings to get to know everyone and to seek input as we prioritize our most pressing issues. Once we have identified areas that need attention, we will get started on resolutions. To begin this process, I would like to set up several teams, composed of community physicians and hospital personnel alike, so that together we can rebuild the bridges of trust between all parties. This goal will be accomplished only if we foster clear and honest communication. I believe that each of you has skills and talents that will help achieve these goals, and I ask for your help in doing so.

Summary

I believe that our medical staff is key to Ventura Hospital's success. Thus, my role as CEO is to enable quality patient care by supporting Ventura's physicians, and indeed all the hospital's employees, in every way I can. Although challenges will inevitably arise, together we can develop innovative solutions that will serve our mission well.

I look forward to working with you in the days ahead!

MEMO TO INITIATE CHANGE

This memo's general purpose is to enable open-mindedness and positive attitudes towards change in the workplace; at the very least, being proactive about discussing change will simmer down the ever-active rumor mill.

More specifically, the purposes of this memo are:

- to frame the forthcoming change as a positive development;
- to explain the new plan "at an appropriate level of detail," (your call);
- to announce a meeting that will further discuss these changes;
- to facilitate cooperation and good will, but also
- to diplomatically acknowledge any major concerns that are likely to exist.

One successful template for composing this memo appears below.

- Express appreciation for your audience.
- Explain the (urgent) need for this change.
- Explain the outcomes/benefits of this change.
- Show that benefits of this change outweigh its costs.
- Visualize harm(s) in not changing.
- Communicate empathy (not sympathy) for audience uncertainty.
- Answer the audience's main concern: "How will this plan affect me?"
- Express appreciation again.
- End on a positive note.

Although I have seen many splendid change memos, and although there are many ways to send these messages, the model on the following page should at least illustrate how the template works.

HEADING

HEADING

HEADING

HEADING

INITIATING CHANGE: MODEL MEMO

The purpose of this memo is to discuss upcoming changes that this department will undergo as part of the broader relocation and reorganization plan initiated by the CEO and the Board of Directors. My goal is to describe these changes and explain how they will affect each of you.

I first want to thank each of you for your fantastic efforts thus far. I know that I can count on your support as we implement a few changes that will increase our productivity while simultaneously increasing the flexibility and predictability of paralegal work schedules. In brief, we plan to transform the paralegal department from a decentralized, one-paralegal-per-attorney system into a central paralegal pool for the entire office.

The Current System

The legal department is populated by highly talented and professional individuals who do credit to themselves and The Company. However, the department's *organization* (for which I am responsible) has become outdated and does not reflect the streamlined, flexible system consistent with the philosophy and organizational structure of a modern corporation. Our current system not only results in uneven workloads among paralegals, but also limits the flexibility of paralegal work schedules because each paralegal's duties are directly tied to the demands of one particular attorney. Thus, some paralegals are overworked while others have little to do.

The Paralegal Pool

After consulting with several of the paralegals and attorneys, I have devised a system that will pool all paralegals and allocate work on an as-needed basis. The main benefit of the system is that the work will be evenly spread among the paralegals. As we all know, it can be difficult for the attorneys to predict their demand for paralegal assistance in advance. However, the "pool approach" will eliminate the need for paralegals' lives to revolve around "their" attorneys. Thus, the office will operate more efficiently while accruing a better work-life balance for the paralegals.

The Transition

I do recognize that this change will require some "getting used to." I also know that many paralegals have developed a great working relationship with their attorneys. However, after a great deal of thought and discussions, I am convinced that the benefits will outweigh the costs. The two primary complaints that I have received from the paralegals over the years have to do with lack of flexibility and uneven workloads. As The Company continues to grow, the expectations laid on this department will increase. By pooling the paralegals, we can increase our overall work throughput time without requiring additional work hours.

This change will take effect when we move to our new building next month. Additional details will be forthcoming. Thank you in advance for your patience and cooperation, as well as for your splendid work ethic and exemplary work products.

THE PROGRESS REPORT MEMO

While progress report memos are quite common and must be as clear and concise as possible, they are so intuitive and easy to write that a model would be superfluous to the template illustration below. For convenience, this explanation uses data from the change model in the previous section. Begin by stating your memo's purpose; then, proceed as directed.

Purpose

This memo tracks the progress of our changes in paralegal assignments.

Brief overview of organization and/or project

As you know, we currently assign paralegal work within a decentralized, one-paralegal-per-attorney system. Although this scheme worked well for a number of years, it has become outdated and inefficient as the company has grown. Too often, some paralegals are overworked while others are relatively idle. Our imminent move to new facilities will provide the space arrangements needed to correct this disparity.

Basic plan

To address its inequities, we are in the process of transforming the decentralized, one-paralegal-per-attorney system into a central paralegal pool for the entire office. Work will be assigned on an as-needed basis.

Progress to date

- All parties have been informed of the change, in writing.
- Paralegals have met for a productive question/answer session.
- Furnishings for the new space have been ordered.
- Most paralegals and attorneys seem positive about the change.

Tasks remaining

- Determine how many paralegals should be assigned to the transition team that will maintain workflow during the move.
- Choose the transition team above.
- Assign "moving duties" to remaining paralegals.
- Allocate workspace in the new facility.

THE ENVIRONMENTAL (S.W.O.T.) ANALYSIS

More and more frequently, managers are asked to produce a "snapshot" environmental analysis, commonly known as the **SWOT**.[7]

Certainly, SWOT analyses can be Michener-like in length; here, however, we focus solely upon memo (1-2 page) length SWOTs.

The basic elements of a SWOT analysis include:

- **Internal** variables within management's control that can either help (strengths) or hinder (weaknesses) corporate goals. These issues include one or more (usually more) of the following:
    - Horizontal Processes
    - Organizational Structure
    - Corporate Culture
    - Management
    - Financial Position
    - Operations
    - Marketing
    - Human Resources
    - Research and Development
    - Information Systems

For example, consider two travel consortiums that have diverse perspectives and corporate cultures. The culture of Company A is focused on its owner's mandate to "spare no expense," while the culture of Company B is more value-oriented.

---

[7] Stahl, M.J., (1996) *Management: Total Quality in a Global Environment.* Oxford, UK: Blackwell. The author hereby and gratefully acknowledges her friend and colleague, Mike Stahl, for teaching her everything she knows about environmental analyses including all data used in this section.

Obviously, different strengths and weakness are more or less important to different companies/industries.

The same is true of variables in the external environment:

- Variables in the **external environment** (opportunities and threats) are not within management's control; nonetheless, these factors directly or indirectly have a significant impact on individual entities and industries alike. These variables include one or more (usually more) of the following trends (or events).
    - Customer Value Trends
    - Social Trends
    - Demographic Trends
    - Economic Trends
    - Technological Trends
    - Regulatory Trends
    - Physical Trends
    - Competitive Trends

A model SWOT memo appears on the following page; bear in mind, however, that it represents the "tip top" of a full-blown SWOT analysis. In short, it is a collection of conclusions – so focus your attention on how the memo is structured, as that part of the model is most valuable to you.

MODEL MEMO: SWOT ANALYSIS

To: Department Heads

From: Angel Michael

Re: Boomer Bikes

Date: 1 January 2012

Corporate Snapshot

Boomer Bikes (BB) was founded in 1967 by a kaput rock band of the same name. The company manufactures motorcycles and accessories (parts and logo clothing), and also owns Midnight Rambler Corporation, a manufacturer of recreational vehicles (RV).

Boomer Bikes competes primarily with the Harley-Davidson Company, as well as with the Japanese *big four*: Honda, the world's largest motorcycle manufacturer; Yamaha, a more diversified manufacturer; plus Suzuki and Kawasaki. Although BB's market share has remained "in the game" over the long haul, it has fluctuated wildly during economic crises.

Fortunately, BB's financial position has made a complete recovery since its net income loss of almost 20 million dollars in 2001. Year ending December 31, 2010, BB's net income was nearly 33 million dollars. The company has shown a 23% increase in income from operations over the past three years. In 2005, the company lowered total debt by $35.1 million. The Company's liquidity is low (current ratio is 1.4:1 and quick ratio is 0.6:1), likely a result of its considerable debt reduction.

Strengths: (in descending order of impact)

1. Its brand is legendary, worldwide.

2. It has utterly loyal customers, with whom BB strengthens relationships by seeking face-to-face input on customer value and product improvement advice.

3. Its motto: "Boomer Bikes or Bust" has led to improved quality, a just-in-time inventory system, and a nearly-flawless supply chain in sales and service. No one wants to see Boomer Bikes "busted."

Principal Weakness

BB's greatest weakness is the Midnight Rambler Corporation. RVs, like motorcycles, are cylindrical luxury items, in an industry plagued by increased operation costs (fuel), declining demand, and decreasing profit margins. Keeping the MRC makes no sense whatsoever.

Best Opportunity

Capture the emerging "boomlet" market – Boomer offspring who already represent 19% of BB's customer base even as BB has virtually ignored them. They are a potential gold mine.

Greatest Threats

Soaring fuel costs and economic downturns are hazardous. Historically BB's overall success has ridden the curve of the U.S. economy, while sales volume has followed fuel prices.

Recommendations

1. Grow the bottom-line: sell the Midnight Rambler division at all costs.

2. Capture the boomlet market with a new line of fuel-efficient bikes whose appearance mimics BB originals. Then flood the social network with rollout events -- and let nostalgia do the rest.

BAD NEWS "BEARERS"

No one likes to be the bearer of bad news. As a manager, you will likely find yourself in that role more often than you might imagine. So, let's look at how to deal with a thankless task. Here, the internet will come in handy. Google "bad news business letters" and you will find a plethora of models and suggestions. My favorite sites:

http://hubpages.com/hub/How-to-Write-a-Bad-News-Business-Letter

http://emedia.leeward.hawaii.edu/hurley/ebc9/2011_weekly_pdfs/docs/bn.pdf

My "take" on bad news memos is that they should be as straightforward as possible. Generally, I recommend something akin to this format:

1. Describe the situation/problem.
2. Be explicit about the likely impact(s) on your audience.
3. Briefly explain how the company is handling the situation.
4. Ask for patience and cooperation.
5. Promise to keep your audience informed.

Most importantly: always be mindful of the message you need to convey. I actually received the following letter many years ago. Even though <u>what</u> one says normally <u>takes a back seat to how one says it</u>, just the opposite is true in this case.

Moral: bad news requires careful handling!

Dear Valued Client:

We regret to inform you that our storage facility burned to the ground on February 4th (last Tuesday). Apparently, it was not fireproof. One result is that you no longer possess the belongings you had stored with us. They no longer exist. Another result is that we are no longer open for business.

You will note that this letter is postmarked from Canada, where we relocated once we realized that our insurance policy had lapsed three days before the fire. We hope you will understand why our move was necessary and will not take it personally.

We will credit your account with your outstanding balance, and we have cancelled your contract so that you can secure storage space elsewhere. We will keep you informed if you need to know anything else,

Regretfully yours,

[Company X]

GUIDELINES FOR E-MAIL

While hundreds of websites and textbooks address this topic, no definitive rules exist. E-delivery remains communication's "wild, wild West" in that it lacks universally-accepted laws and orders.

Thus, perhaps the most important rule regarding e-communication of all kinds is to conform to expectations within your workplace. The guidelines below are widely accepted as simple common sense:

- Be succinct. If your document is longer than one page, attach it to your email as a readable file. In the email body, then, write a one-sentence purpose for your having sent it, and if appropriate, ask for a specific response from the recipient.
- Avoid hitting REPLY TO ALL unless the situation demands it.
- Use list serve functions with careful forethought.
- Avoid "flameouts" – email's most commonly identified problem! Avoid verbal attacks in email; they may prove to be libelous!
- Avoid overuse of upper case letters as this practice is generally perceived as written shouting.
- Make certain your email is "eye scannable;" avoid walls of text.
- Write, edit, proofread, and spellcheck email just as you would any written document; that's exactly what email is.
- Avoid forwarding/sending chain letters and the like while at work.
- Remember: most organizations "own" their email; it is neither private nor protected by law. Your email could end up being printed and/or circulated elsewhere. Compose with care.
- Likewise, do not use your workplace email for personal correspondence.

CHAPTER VII: DOCUMENTS FOR JOB SEEKERS

A battleship would sink under the weight of books, workbooks, handouts, and everything else that is available to help organize and compose resumes, vitas, cover-letters, and every other job-search document one could imagine. Not only that, but college and other career centers are readily available to most people, not to mention the ever-growing cadre of resume specialists who will craft personalized documents – normally for not-so-small a fee.

Thus, our goal here is to confirm the validity of what you likely already know, then to throw in a few tricks that may give you the proverbial "edge" next time you need it.

CHRONOLOGICAL RESUMES

Virtually everyone within shouting distance of any business or professional venture is familiar with, and likely has used, this time-honored format. Virtually everyone understands it. Virtually everyone accepts it. Virtually everyone is bored by it – but it's the "devil everyone knows."

Am I "dissing" traditional resumes? **NO.** Please refrain from waving this page in your career coach's face as if the chronological resume were a week-old pork chop. What I AM suggesting is that you find a way to make your traditional resume stand out in a crowd.

Here's an example. As you know, most resumes are scanned and analyzed to see how closely the resume matches the position sought. "Clouding" is one way you can see what a scan of your resume would emphasize.

First, go to www.wordle.net Copy your resume into the "cloud maker" as directed. Voila! You'll see yourself as scanners see you.

Then, create another "cloud" using the job description you are gunning for. Compare the two. Does your resume scan match the job description scan? If not, edit your resume so that your cloud words better match.

As an example, the cloud below was created from a resume we'll examine in the next section[8]. How does the cloud describe the applicant?

---

[8] Naturally, you'll be able to see your words better when the cloud is sized appropriately

You should "cloud test" every job you apply for; then, tweak your resume to match the job description. Sure, that's a lot of work. But it beats standing in the unemployment line.

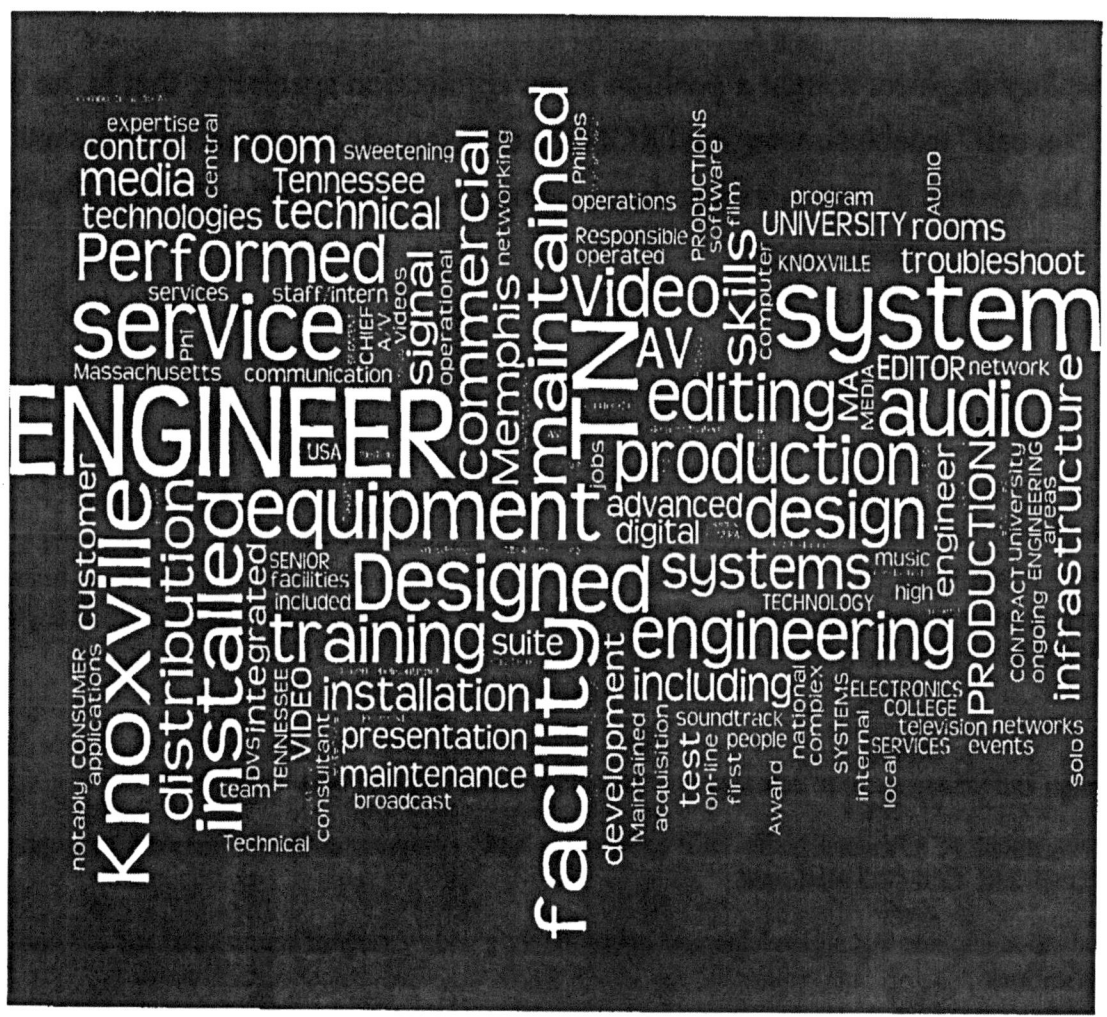

THE SKILLS-FOCUSED RESUME

Today more than ever, recruiters want to know what skills sets you bring to the table, regardless of the positions you have held. Thus, you may want to consider adding a skills-focused resume to your portfolio, whether you are seeking your first career step, your last, or somewhere in between.

If you are a seasoned professional (akin to the audio-video engineer whose "career cloud" we saw on the previous page), then you doubtless want to emphasize experiences that are most relevant to the position you seek.

Our exemplary engineer sought a position as an application specialist; that is, he wanted to be the "on call" troubleshooter for TROMP technologies. To emphasize relevant skills, he began his resume by summarizing them, being careful to mention his familiarity with TROMP and similar technology:

PROFESSIONAL EXPERIENCE

SKILLS SUMMARY

Comprehensive knowledge of networked communication technologies and integrated media systems; expertise in TROMP and COLGIG platforms as well as in AV system planning, design, installation, testing, and maintenance; exceptional people skills; 25+ years' experience in AV applications engineering with demonstrated enthusiasm for and advanced proficiencies in:

- Design and management of complex multi-media systems and networks
- Management of advanced audio DSP technology and computer/audio/AV networking supported by TROMP and COLGIG platforms
- Production engineering, supervision, and operation for a wide variety of commercial and consumer media applications
- Outstanding customer service, notably for users of A/V and integrated systems technologies
- Leadership, communication, teamwork, and people skills, notably in high stress situations
- Technical training and presentation skills
- Comprehensive computer application skills including MS Office

He followed up this summary with a fairly traditional chronology, then ended with his education/credentials. (See Appendix B). The format above is somewhat unique because it not only summarizes the applicant's skills but also emphasizes his strengths.

Ironically, this format is often helpful when the applicant has useful skills sets but lacks considerable experience – such as a new college grad or someone who wants to make a career path change. For example, "Bob Goodman" has considerable experience in the entertainment industry, but he now wants to change career paths and work in hospitality. He used the skills format to help make this transition; his resume begins:

SKILLS SUMMARY

Proven excellence in management, leadership, multi-tasking, and problem-solving skills. Expert-level proficiency with computers and numerous software applications, with fast learning curve for new software/technology. Uncommonly intelligent and sociable. Keen desire to begin a new career in the hotel/hospitality industry where my demonstrated enthusiasm for life and strengths in the follow areas can add considerable value to the corporate mission:

- o Excellent leadership, communication, teamwork and people skills, in high stress situations
- o Ability to appropriately deal with people in all strata of society
- o Proven expertise in providing elite customer services to A-list clientele
- o An exceptional track record of success in sales/marketing
- o Proficiency in budgeting, cost reporting, contract and other accounting skills
- o The ability to learn quickly, follow procedures and represent my employer with pride and professionalism.
- o A strong desire to begin a new career in the hotel industry, specifically for long-term opportunity to grow "up the ladder" with *****

Finally, note "Jon Doer's" resume on the next page. He has strong skills, so he puts his best foot forward (skills/personal attributes) and his weakest details last – including the fact that he lacks a college degree.

email address **JON DOER** 111.111.1234

Versatile, energetic, and uniquely qualified customer service specialist with a passion for the hospitality industry seeks challenging career track position

CUSTOMER SERVICE & ADMINISTRATIVE EXPERIENCE

- Provided executive assistance to c-level physicians and academic administrators
- Organized catering and transportation services for executive training programs
- Facilitated distance learning seminars for physicians/executives
- Managed concierge services for groups of 35-100 executives in residence
- Developed multi-tasking expertise in fast-paced, high stress environment
- Organized logistics for residential seminars: travel, hotel, F&B, and special events
- Managed inventory: created database for tracking and procurement
- Supervised permanent and temporary F&B employees
- Supported marketing and customer relations campaigns
- Managed various accounting functions: reconciliation, research, and budgeting

INTEGRATED TECHNOLOGY EXPERIENCE

- Developed expertise in using all MSOffice products
- Proficient in most commonly-used software applications
- Designed numerous databases and websites
- Certified Apple Product Professional
- Tutored in and supplied software support for both Mac OSX and Windows
- Multimedia A/V troubleshooting and servicing
- Telecommunication support in distance learning environment

PERSONAL ATTRIBUTES

- Excellent written/oral communication skills
- Exemplary work ethic; will do what it takes to get the job done
- Equally effective working in teams or individually
- Available immediately; willing to travel

EMPLOYMENT HISTORY

<u>Executive Assistant & Client Services Specialist</u> (dates)
[Company, City & State]
<u>Customer Service Specialist</u> (dates)
[Company, City & State]
<u>Food & Beverage Server</u> – dates
[Company, City & State]
<u>Shift Manager</u> –dates
[Company, City & State]

EDUCATION

- Graduate, Disney Traditions Training, Orlando FL (date)
- University of Tennessee, Knoxville TN (date) Completed [hrs] coursework in [major]

COVER LETTERS

What hasn't been said about cover letters? My favorite comment was printed in a newspaper article that admonished writers to perfect their grammar and mechanics:

Recruiters are searching for reasons to eliminate you.

Don't give it to them by writing a cover letter.

While humorous on several levels, this poorly-communicated message contains a kernel of truth: *A good cover letter can make the reader want to meet you; a bad cover letter usually has the opposite effect.*

Use whatever resources you have in composing cover letters, including services offered by well-connected career counselors. That being said, I have found three tried-and-true "golden" cover letter rules:

- ✓ Above all, eliminate grammar and mechanical errors. I once saw a cover letter addressed to *Proctor & Gamble* (Procter being correct). If you can't spell the company's name, you don't need to work there.

- ✓ Read the letter aloud. Be sure that what you say is what you mean.

- ✓ Make certain that every letter you send is customized and "form fitted" to the job you're applying for. While you can use some of your own "boilerplate," each letter should be different, just as each job description is different. The letter body on the following page targets a Research Associate position at DIGG Data:

BODY OF COVER LETTER PITCHED TO SPECIFIC POSITION[9]

As a **versatile, results-oriented social scientist with exemplary research skills and experience, I believe I am the Research Associate that you are seeking for DIGG Data.** Please consider my:

- **Graduate-level research experience.** While I was an undergraduate, at Ivy University, I was Dr. Name Researcher's primary assistant for 7 semesters (2007-2009). I worked independently and with faculty teams to gather, code, and interpret data for grant-funded, policy-oriented research. I also presented reports/ findings and authored or co-authored monographs. These experiences fine-tuned my innately **strong qualitative and quantitative analytical skills, particularly in survey, ethnographic and interview oriented research,** while requiring that I be **proactive, self-directed, detail-oriented, discerning and creative.**

- Unique **administrative experience.** My diverse experiences as an administrative assistant are more than commensurate with 5+ years in a similar support role. For a year prior to my move to New York (May 2009-2010), and continuing to the present in a remote capacity, I have worked as a professional event planner -- designing, organizing, and implementing high-profile events for various entities and individuals, primarily for charitable causes.

- **Strong communication, organizational and problem-solving skills.** These enabled me to serve for five years (2001-2005) as a scheduled volunteer assistant to the Director of Community Relations at St. Paul's Children's Hospital, Dr. Jane Rose. Dr. Rose often compared my administrative expertise to that of a seasoned professional. I encourage you to contact her at 000-000-0000.

- **Exemplary people skills.** The experiences listed above, combined with a plethora of leadership roles and community service activities, have enhanced my innately strong **interpersonal skills.** My orientation supervisor often described me as an **effective team player** and servant-leader.

- **Commitment to excellence.** I graduated *Magna Cum Laude* from Ivy University with a B.A. in sociology (2009). I was a four-year Presidential Scholar, maintained a 3.79 GPA, minored in both French and business, and participated in numerous activities that included a variety of artistic endeavors as well as student governance and community service. In recognition of these achievements, Ivy awarded me the *Annie Sullivan Prize for Unique Achievements.*

I live and work in Manhattan and would love to meet with you to discuss the many ways I may be of value to DIGG Data. Thank you in advance for your consideration.

The words in bold type above appeared in the job posting as well as in the cover letter. Using the job description's language links you to the position – especially when our friend, the scanner, dissects your documents into word clusters!

---

[9] Some career specialists may not agree with this approach. Compare several models and see what you "resonate" with the most, all things considered.

CHAPTER VIII: GUIDELINES FOR LONGER REPORTS[10]

(model for placement of main heading)

Definition and Format

(model for placement of secondary heading)

<u>Definition</u> (model for placement of tertiary heading)

These guidelines will govern all papers that are designated as "reports" and/or are greater than four pages in length. If in doubt about formatting issues, ask for clarification.

<u>Margins</u>

Set margins at 1-inch. If the report is bound, set the left margin at 1.5"

<u>Pagination</u>

Do not number the first page. Number all following pages either ½ inch from the top right or ½ inch from the bottom center. Some companies prefer that you indicate the order and scope of the paper by writing Page x of y (e.g. Page 2 of 20); most do not.

<u>Spacing</u>

Reports should be double-spaced throughout, and paragraphs should be indented (unlike a memo). NOTE, however, that Executive Summaries attached to long reports should be single-spaced and should follow traditional memo guidelines.

Reference page(s) may be single-spaced or double-spaced.

---

[10] This arrangement is only one of many possibilities. See page 29.

Quotations in excess of two typed lines of text should be set in ½ inch from each margin and may be either single or double-spaced. It is permissible to italicize the indented quotation.

<u>Headings</u>

Note appropriate placement of headings as indicated in this chapter's text: primary, secondary, tertiary, and beyond.

<u>Listings</u>

1. Indent numbered lists approximately ½ inch from the *body text's* left margin.

2. Single space items that are longer than one line.

3. Indent second and following lines underneath the first WORD above, not underneath, the number.

4. In a double-spaced document, double-space between list items.

Report Contents and Order

<u>Title Page.</u>

Center on one sheet:

Title of report (all caps, all bold)

Author

Date

Add other items as requested

Table of Contents

List the headings exactly as they appear in the report body. If the report is fewer than 25 pages, list all levels of headings, indicating their relevance to each other via indentation.

In a very long report, you may choose one heading level and put only the headings at that level and above in the Table of Contents.

Executive Summary

This document follows the Table of Contents and should be one page, single-spaced. Some companies require longer E-Summaries, so please ask if in doubt.

Main Body of the Report

- Write in paragraph form.
- Use bullets and lists as appropriate.
- Note the general order and guidelines below.

    Introduction (model for placement of a fourth-level heading)

    - Orient the reader to the report.
    - Use both a statement of purpose and of scope.

    Body of the Report

    Write as assigned; present and interpret data and/or analyze causes, make recommendations. Some firms prefer that recommendations be placed at the beginning of the report; a few do not. Always ask.

    Conclusion

    Briefly summarizes main points; if recommendations aren't made earlier (rare), then they are combined with this section.

Citations/Documentation

Although most academic journals use APA format or a similar form of internal citation, footnotes are preferable in business reports because they leave the manuscript "cleaner" and therefore more readable. Thus, the following citation formats are suggested; however, if your supervisor prefers internal citations, models of these may be found in any good reference text.

Footnotes

Footnotes are numbered within the text with references located at the bottom of the page whereon the footnote appears. MS WORD will format these references automatically. Footnote format:

Books, first reference

Linda Lyle, *Writing Strategically,* (1999), 24.

(author, work, year, page)

Books, subsequent

Lyle, 445.

If Lyle has more than one book referenced, the title must be repeated when necessary to indicate appropriate reference.

Periodicals, first reference

Linda Lyle, "Strategic Writing," *Communication Quarterly* (2004): 333.

or if author is unknown:

"Strategic Writing," *Communication Quarterly* (2004): 333.

Other

For print sources other than books or periodicals, include author or source, name of article, date and page number(s). For online sources, a URL is normally sufficient.

Note that footnotes may also be used to make brief personal comments regarding information in the text.

Endnotes

Endnotes will contain the same information except that all references will be located on an ENDNOTES page, placed just prior to the Bibliography.

Bibliography

Literally dozens of formats are used in bibliographical listings. Regardless of which format you choose, all pertinent information in the list below should be included:

    Author(s)

    Date of publication

    Source title

    Publication information

    Books: City: Publisher

    Periodicals: Publication, Volume, page numbers

    Online: Name of article, URL

Tables[11]

Informal Tables

Informal tables are used to make small bundles of information within a paragraph more readable; these need no title, nor do they need to be boxed or labeled because their meaning should flow from the text in which they are embedded. Informal tables usually contain 2-4 rows and no more than 3-4 columns. Indent informal tables ½ inch from both text margins.

Formal Tables

- Set off from the text with spacing or (more commonly) by boxing the contents.
- Place titles ABOVE tables
- Number tables with Roman numerals (TABLE IX: MBA GRADES 2009)
- Place captions below the numeral/title
- Split tables of more than one page into more distinct categories (usually); ask the assigning professor if in doubt.

Exhibits

- Every visual should contain six components:

- A title which describes the visual (tells the story)

- A clear indication of what the data are

- Clearly labeled units

- Labels or legends that identify axes, colors, symbols, etc.

- The source of the data noted at the bottom of the visual

- The source of the visual, if reproduced

Note that you need to use the correct exhibit format for the story you want to tell.

---

[11] Keene, M., et.al., (1995) *A Short Guide to Business Writing.*

Appendices[12]

An appendix is any section that conveniently conveys information too bulky to be included in the body of the paper: maps, large technical diagrams and/or busy charts, computations, test data, lists, and the like.

Appendices are

- usually lettered rather than numbered (i.e. Appendix A)
- arranged in alphabetical order
- listed in the Table of Contents

---

[12] Markel (1996) *Technical Communication.*

APPENDIX A

"911" EDITING: USEFUL IN EMERGENCIES

<u>What is "911" editing?</u>

Nearly everyone is guilty of sloppy editing at one time or another. But many are stumped before they start to edit their first draft; they know what they mean, and they think that's what they wrote.

"911" editing is a conglomeration of "emergency" editing tricks that will clear up wordy undergrowth considerably, and will hopefully lead the user to discover even more ways in which to revise and rehabilitate written work.

<u>Lose the Lard</u>

This idea originated with Lanham's Paramedic Method of editing (Google it if you're interested). This method's goal is to produce as "lean" a paper as possible. Lanham's method has two key components:

1. Where possible, convert all prepositional phrases into adjectives. For example, instead of writing "the goal of this method," write, "this method's goal." This one step can sometimes cut the word count by 30+ percent.

2. Convert all "state of being" verbs into active constructions. For example, change "There are six boats in the slip," to "The slip holds six boats."

The word-count difference between the raw version and the edited version(s) is known as the "lard factor" (LF). So, if your paper's LF is 50% then you (theoretically) have twice as many words as you need.

Note the progressively leaner versions of the simple message below:

DRAFT 1:

The purpose of this communication at this time is to let you know where the emphasis is going to be, and to encourage each of you to start thinking about how you can contribute to its process. [37 wds]

> **Comment**: You might think this sentence made more sense in its context, but it didn't. Before we trash it, however notice: (1) the "Simpson's dog" opening - *The purpose of this communication at this time is*; and (2) how the general terms mutate from *purpose* to *emphasis* to *process* without reason; (3) the unfocused verbs and suppressed verbals: *purpose, communicate, know, emphasize, encourage, think, contribute.*

This mess has so many problems that you must rewrite rather than revise:

Revision 1: *This memo describes our policy; please start thinking about how we can implement it. [14/37 = 45% LF]*

Revision 2: *Please consider how we can implement the policy described in this memo. [12/37 = 68% LF]*

Revision 3: *Can we implement this memo's policy proposal? [81% LF]*

Sometimes, the message's intended focus is skewed by a skimpy revision (81%); sometimes it's not. But the point here is that merely applying the two "911 rules" listed above will kick-start your revision process – and possibly finish it altogether.

Moral: Although well-written sentences can (and should) be lengthy on occasion, generally a first draft has a LF of between 30-50%.

Caveat: Avoid creating "playschool" sentences and/or choppy rhythms in your zeal to edit.

In short , strike a perfect balance! ☺

APPENDIX B
COMPLETE PROFESSIONAL SKILLS RESUME

NAME

(865) 000-0000

email@aol.com

PROFESSIONAL EXPERIENCE

SKILLS SUMMARY

Comprehensive knowledge of networked communication technologies and integrated media systems; expertise in AV system planning, design, installation, testing, and maintenance; exceptional people skills; 25+ years' experience in AV applications engineering; demonstrated enthusiasm for and expertise in:

- Design and management of complex multi-media systems and networks
- Management of advanced audio DSP technology and computer/audio/AV networking
- Production engineering and operation for commercial and consumer media applications
- Outstanding customer service, notably for users of A/V and integrated systems technologies
- Leadership, communication, teamwork, and people skills, notably in high stress situations
- Technical training and presentation skills; numerous computer application skills

2008-present **NAME OF INSTITUTION, City & State**

SR. TECHNOLOGIST II & CHIEF AV ENGINEER

- Manage, maintain, and advance audiovisual infrastructure and associated network and engineering operations that use XXX-driven technologies to provide, among other advanced capabilities, high definition multi-image/source projection, capture/retrieval of rich media presentations, video conferencing, and electronic collaboration for 22 classrooms, 33 team rooms, assorted public areas, special function spaces, tech services control rooms and production areas
- Troubleshoot, diagnose and resolve complex system performance issues
- Monitor and troubleshoot AV system tie-ins to facility's networking and server operations
- Initiate and implement upgrades for all media delivery systems in the facility
- Provide extensive training and user-centered customer service to a client base whose technical skills range from extremely limited to exceptionally advanced
- Selected as one of three finalists for Innovation Award during first year of service
- Received *White Glove Service Award, 2010*

2002-2008 **NAME OF INSTITUTION, City & State**

MANAGER, TECHNOLOGY AND TELECOMMUNICATIONS SERVICES

- Responsible for all technical services, infrastructure, and operational systems including all A/V distribution and presentation; internal and client-serving computer networks; PBX based phone and ISDN service; and centralized lighting design and control

- Maintain, troubleshoot, and repair all system hardware; troubleshoot, backup, and update all system software. Initiated and completed several revisions in initial system designs to improve overall functionality

- Primary contact for all technical service needs and consultant to outside contractors

- Liaison with local and national network crews to coordinate broadcast events on site

- Graphic creation and presentation on marquees and internal plasma screens

- Conducted periodic staff/intern training in basic service procedures

1999-2001 NAME OF INSTITUTION, City & State

SIGNAL SYSTEMS ENGINEER

- Designed, installed and maintained central signal distribution system for digital set-top box development facility. Responsibilities included signal room design, equipment acquisition, installation of cabling infrastructure, ongoing operational upgrading/ maintenance, and staff/ intern training

- Designed/implemented software QA test plans for commercial digital receivers

- Performed service engineering and customer support, including installation and training for product verification equipment in Taiwan production facility

1995-1999 NAME OF INSTITUTION, City & State

SENIOR ENGINEER, DIGITAL VIDEO COMMUNICATIONS SYSTEMS

- Designed, installed, and maintained a central signal distribution system for a new digital electronics development facility: responsibilities included infrastructure wiring (fiber, coax, twisted pair), signal room design, equipment acquisition, and ongoing operation/upgrading/ maintenance

- First service engineer in the USA for [X's] professional MPEG transmission equipment; installed first U.S. system at WIT in Washington, D.C. (10/95)

SENIOR ENGINEER, CONSUMER ELECTRONICS

- Project engineer on Philips WebTV design team; responsible electrical engineer for WebEye feature of second-generation television internet browser

- Technical consultant for commercial TV advertising

- Designed and installed distribution and test facilities for DTV development centers

- Planned and implemented technical relocation of distribution and test facilities from Knoxville, TN to Briarcliff, NY and Palo Alto, CA

1992-2000	**NAME OF INSTITUTION, City & State**
	ADJUNCT INSTRUCTOR, PRODUCTION TECHNOLOGY

- Taught video and audio production/technology courses
- Designed audio curriculum and specified equipment for PSTCC-VPT program

1994-1995	**NAME OF INSTITUTION, City & State**
	CONTRACT VIDEO/AUDIO ENGINEER

- Installed and maintained video editing suites
- Supervised production dubbing
- Performed miscellaneous freelance production jobs

1990-1994	**NAME OF INSTITUTION, City & State**
	CONTRACT VIDEO ENGINEER

- Designed, installed, an maintained video post-production and audio sweetening rooms

1988-1990	**NAME OF INSTITUTION, City & State**
	CHIEF AUDIO ENGINEER ON-LINE EDITOR AND ASSISTANT VIDEO ENGINEER

- Responsible for audio integrity on all corporate broadcast and taped productions
- Designed, installed, maintained and operated 16-track audio sweetening room
- Assisted in design, installation, and maintenance of on-line, multi-format (Betacam & 1") editing suite and live production control room in fully integrated facilities

1987-88	**NAME OF INSTITUTION, City & State**
	MASTER CONTROL OPERATOR AND SEGMENT EDITOR

- Performed on-air switching and program editing
- Satellite programming and film-to-tape transfer

1986-87   **NAME OF INSTITUTION, City & State**

STAFF AUDIO ENGINEER; LEAD VIDEO ENGINEER & EDITOR

- Session engineering, mixing and editing
- Maintained facility equipment, including Neve, Trident, & MCI consoles
- Designed, installed, maintained and operated 3/4" editing suite
- Set up synchronization link between video suite and recording studio

1984-86   **NAME OF INSTITUTION, City & State**

AV PRODUCTION & MAINTENANCE ENGINEER

- Engineered demo recordings
- Maintained facility audio and video equipment
- Performed various production jobs on national and local commercials and music videos

EDUCATION

1995   **B.S.E. in ELECTRICAL/COMPUTER ENGINEERING**

University of Tennessee, Knoxville

1990   **LOWELL INSTITUTE AT M.I.T.**

Massachusetts Institute of Technology, Cambridge, Massachusetts

1986   **B.F.A. in COMMERCIAL MUSIC/RECORDING ENGINEERING**

MINORS in FILM/VIDEO PRODUCTION & ECONOMICS

Memphis State University, Memphis, Tennessee

Phi Kappa Phi & Golden Key Honor Society

1980-83   **UNIVERSITY OF WISCONSIN, Madison, Wisconsin**

Acknowledgements

So many people to thank, so little space to thank them!

First and foremost, thanks to the University of Tennessee's College of Business Administration, where for the past two decades I have had unique and wonderful opportunities to use my vital powers along lines of excellence in a life affording them scope. The ancient Greeks were right: such endeavors are the essence of happiness. Thus, to my friends and colleagues in the CBA, including and especially my ultra-supportive husband Kerry Roehr, I owe an immeasurable debt of gratitude. Thank you for "making" all my days!

*This book owes its existence to Tom Brown, whose idea it was to begin with; it was also influenced by the students I have taught for the past 38 years, many of whom have remained part of my extended family. All of them are special – but none more so than "my" UTK MBA Class of 2008. Greg, Ned, Mike, Bobby, Jess, Chase, Paige, Lindsay, Ravi, Amanda, Jared, James, **all of you**! You kept me going, kiddos; you reminded me to keep living on the edge so I wouldn't take up too much room; you continue to be an inspiration. What a journey we've had together!*

That's why this one's for you. Live long and prosper.

Linda Lyle

Knoxville, Tennessee

May 2011

About the Author

Dr. Linda Lyle has taught communication studies in the University of Tennessee's full-time MBA program since 1992 and has served as a Core Faculty member for UT's Physicians' Executive MBA program since 2004. Previously, she was a travel industry executive, as well as an award-winning high school forensics coach, English teacher, and journalism advisor.

A former Executive Director of the Tennessee Communication Association, she has served two terms as its President. She was named the state's *Outstanding Communication Educator* in 2005. The UTK MBA class selected her as its *Outstanding Professor* in 2008, when she was also one of three finalists for the East Tennessee YWCA's *Tribute to Women in Education Award*.

Dr. Lyle became an activist with the Michael J. Fox Foundation for Parkinson's Research when she was diagnosed with PD in 2003; subsequently, she earned recognition as a *Team Fox MVP* in 2007 and 2009. She lives in Knoxville, Tennessee with her husband, Kerry Roehr, an AV systems engineer, and their pit bull terrier, Bash. Dr. Lyle loves to travel, to dabble in daughter Madison Lyleroehr's musical endeavors -- and she is still writing the next great American novel in her spare time.

Bibliography & Selected Readings

Griffin, Jack (1998)   How to Say It at Work. Prentice Hall, USA

http://www.collegeboard.com/prod_downloads/writingcom/writing-ticket-to-work.pdf

http://www.editorialservice.com/11ways.html

http://www.unc.edu/depts/wcweb/handouts/brainstorming.html

http://hubpages.com/hub/How-to-Write-a-Bad-News-Business-Letter

http://emedia.leeward.hawaii.edu/hurley/ebc9/2011_weekly_pdfs/docs/bn.pdf

http://www.wordle.net

http://www.scribd.com/doc/2664713/Associated-Press-AP-Style-Guide-the-basics

http://owl.english.purdue.edu/owl/resource/592/1/

Keene, M., et.al., (1995) A Short Guide to Business Writing. Prentice Hall, USA.

Markel, M., (1996) Technical Communication. St. Martin's Press, Canada.

Stahl, M.J., (1996) Management: Total Quality in a Global Environment. Blackwell, UK.

www.lyle.vpnet.com

CPSIA information can be obtained at www.ICGtesting.com
Printed in the USA
LVOW090115190912

299235LV00001BA/2/P